Why You Su

Do you suck at golf? Do you know someone who does? While written in a tongue-in-cheek style, *Why You Suck at Golf* is an informative and educational manual chronicling the most common mistakes golfers make when playing this wondrous game. From arriving too late for your tee time, to trying to keep your head still, if there is a common, easily correctible mistake a golfer makes it is in this book. Over fifty chapters, each discuss a mistake and how to correct it.

So whether you want to have a little dig at the golfaholic among your friends or family, or are serious about eradicating shot-costing mistakes in your game, *"Why You Suck at Golf"* is a must-read. Written by Teaching Professional Clive Scarff, author of the #1 ranked *"Hit Down Dammit!"* golf instruction book (also available on Amazon, Barnes & Noble, iTunes).

I bought it for a friend, and then ended up reading it and getting my own copy...
Brian M.

OMG I laughed - but it was all true!
Dave W.

I bought this book for my husband. At first he was mad, later he kissed me!
Sharon S.

One of the funniest, but very well detailed and explanatory books out on the market!!!! Lisa G.

Why You Suck at Golf
Ravenrock Publishing Inc
1120 Fabrick Drive
Qualicum Beach, BC, Canada V9K 1M9
COPYRIGHT © 2011   Clive Scarff

DISTRIBUTED BY RAVENROCK PUBLISHING
ELECTRONIC EDITION: 2011, Canada
NATIONAL LIBRARY OF CANADA CATALOGUING IN PUBLICATION

Clive Scarff
Why You Suck at Golf / Clive Scarff

I. Golf Instruction II. Golf Humour   III. Golf Tips
ISBN 978-1-927069-06-6 Hardback
ISBN 978-1-927069-05-9 Paperback
ISBN 978-1-927069-04-2 Electronic Format (PDF/ePub)
www.ravenrockpublishing.com

Why You Suck at Golf
Contents

Introduction

One of the (many) unique things about golf is not just how many players suck at it, but how many people will tell you they suck at it. Almost brazenly. If I had a dollar for every time I mentioned to someone that I play golf, only to hear, "*Oh, I suck at golf!*" I would be extremely well off.

It is very odd. If you mention to someone you are going to play a little pick-up ball, you do not normally hear in reply, "Oh, I suck at basketball!" Mention you are going down to the local tennis club and the response is not generally, "Tennis? I'm awful at tennis!" The other oddity in connection to golf is how often "Oh, I suck at golf!" is followed by, "But I love it!" Imagine telling a potential suitor, "Sex? Oh well, I'm terrible, but boy I sure like it!" Good luck with that.

Here we have a sport that a great many people love, yet admittedly suck at, but they keep on trying. You do not find that in bullfighting. Or tower diving. Nope, just golf. That wonderful, crazy, seemingly mystical, often addictive and very unique game of golf.

Interestingly, the seeming uniqueness of golf plays into why so many people do suck at it. They see it as different from other sports, and so they treat it differently from other sports. They do things in the game of golf they would *never* do in another sport, and then wonder why they do not play it as well as they do the other sports. Hmmm. Connection?

This book, *"Why You Suck at Golf"* aims certainly to have some fun with the fact that so many people do struggle with the game, but truthfully, the deep down objective is to point out a great many of the foibles that golfers engage in when approaching the sport, so they can stop doing those "foiblish" things. And, stop sucking.

Whether trying to make an athletic manoeuvre without moving your head, practicing something you do fourteen times in a game and ignoring something you do forty times, claiming lessons are too expensive while leaning on an $800 driver, sprinting from the car to the first tee and then claiming a bad first hole ruined the round, giving your new swing a whole week to prove itself, or aiming with your feet rather than your clubface, golfers do some odd things in the game they claim they suck at. We will explore a great many things that you can change – easily –overnight, so you can gain positive results in your game without getting into swing mechanics or muscle memory one iota.

Join me, and my hapless golf buddy/scapegoat "Bogart" as we reveal why so many people suck at such a succulent game. If you enjoy the read along the way, that would not suck at all.

Clive.

Tee Time

Bogart

Bogart is a friend of mine. He is an average golfer at best, and if that is not an oxymoron I do not know what is. Truth is, he sucks.

Bogart has a lot of money. That he likes to give to Charity. Charity is another friend of ours and she just loves playing golf with Bogart. She has never lost to him.

Bogart has the best equipment. Top of the line. His driver cost more than most people's sets but he has never spent a dime on lessons. I think he plays with me to mooch for free advice, which I would say was cheesy but I play with my accountant and stock broker for the same reason.

I am embarrassed that Bogart has started dressing like Rickie Fowler, yet relieved he has stopped dressing like John Daly. Bogart's swing is not perfect, far from it, but nor is it the real cause of his high scores. Bogart simply makes a host of practical, psychological, and mental mistakes each and every time he plays which heap strokes onto his score like syrup on pancakes.

If Bogart would just take the time to address the issues outlined in this book, he could drop shots in bunches with virtually no change to his swing. Guess what he is getting for Christmas?

Let's get on with the book…

You Arrive Too Close to Your Tee Time

Hockey players arrive a good hour or more before a game. Tennis players nearly always rally before playing an actual game, and all recreational baseball players I know throw the ball around and do some batting practice prior to "Play ball!".

Meet Bogart, our well intentioned golfer. Time: 1:10. Tee time: 1:14. We hear screeching tires as a car pulls into the golf club parking lot the way a police cruiser might at a donut store. The trunk pops open. Bogart leaps out of the vehicle and runs to the back, yanking a bag of clubs from within. He would check to make sure all his clubs are in the bag, but there is no time. He slams the trunk shut and begins to run, but just as quickly makes an about-face and returns to the trunk again. Damn, where are the keys? There they are; the trunk opens, and Bogart reaches in and retrieves his golf shoes. He kicks off his loafers and, clubs on his back, bends over to put his Footjoys on. Luckily only one club falls out of the bag, and the tying of the laces can wait until he reaches the tee. Which he does, panting like a bloodhound with exercise-induced asthma.

He makes his apologies to his playing partners but they cannot hear him, as he is talking into his shoes as he laces them up. Tied, and his turn to hit. Good news! Despite all this rushing, his drive does not go out of bounds. It only went 50 yards mind you, but at least it did not go out of bounds. Oh dear. His second shot went out of bounds, trying to pound it to make up for the 50 yard blooper. The interesting thing? He would not tell you now, because he is too frazzled to talk, but catch him another time and Bogart will tell you: he plays golf to relax.

You Put Your Sunscreen On Too Late

The best time to put your sunscreen on, before playing golf, is just before you leave home, or immediately you get out of the car upon arrival at the golf club.

Bogart has a habit of getting to the first tee, looking up

at the big yellow thing in the sky, and then realizing he ought to slap some sunscreen on. He then proceeds to hit a pretty important shot – the first one of the day – with hands lathered in slippery, creamy, sunscreen. And don't worry, I make sure I never stand anywhere near him when he does that.

You Don't Practice Putting Before Playing

There is no getting around this, putting is half the game. Literally. Each stroke of the putter costs you an entire shot. A missed short putt is empirically just as negative to your score as a completely whiffed tee shot. In fact it may even be worse, as the whiffed tee shot did not move further from the hole, versus the missed two footer that may now be a four-footer.

Why then does Bogart dash to the driving range to jam in a quick bucket of balls before playing and completely ignore the putting green? The act of dashing and rushing could actually be detrimental to his tempo when he imminently tees off. And if he did hit the opening hole in two, what good is that if he three- putts?

The practice putting green is *usually* handy to the first tee, a perfect place to practice your stroke, listen for your name to be called, and then a leisurely walk to get your round started.

I have left the most important argument to last: the

speeds of putting greens vary from course to course, and on the same course vary from day to day, week to week. Practicing putting before you play gives you vital information as to the speed and roll of the greens you are about to play on, and that information alone can prevent many wasted putts (putts = strokes) in your round.

You Rush a Bucket Before Teeing Off

I have been guilty of this on more than one occasion, but it is still wrong. Bogart has ten minutes before his tee time. Not wanting to play cold, he buys a small bucket of balls, jogs to the driving range, and whacks them away, resembling a gattling gun far more than Ernie Els.

Why go hit 40 very quick shots right before a game you are likely to play slowly? The very act of banging off 40 shots in ten minutes will increase your tempo to an untenable degree. Unless you are about to play speed golf, this will do more harm to your game than good *and* you are out five bucks for the bucket of balls.

You would be better served to *walk* over to the range and hit six (yes, six) smooth shots and walk back. To the putting green. Or better yet! Show up an hour before your tee time and hit a relaxed small bucket of balls for 30 minutes, and then walk to the putting green for some putting practice. But this is only if you want to play better golf, of course.

You Don't Pack a Snack

It seems simple. After all, we know we need food for energy. Yet, I would say it is one in ten I ever see pack any kind of snack when playing golf.

Sure, many of you grab a dog at the turn if the halfway shack is open. But many do not even then, and that shack is not always open. It just makes sense to put some sustenance in that golf bag of yours (take twenty or thirty balls out if you need to make room).
Graze; have a bite (or swig) of something every two or three holes to maintain a consistent energy level throughout your round. Nuts, bananas, grapes, granola or even chocolate bars, roast pork, something. And do not forget water and/or an energy drink. It may even save you $15 at the turn.

You Don't Carry a Rule Book

They are inexpensive, they are small, they fit in your golf bag. You cannot look up a rule when you need to if you do not have a rule book (or at least a cheat sheet). Get a rule book and save strokes.

You Don't Play With People You Like

While I am the first to concede you ought to learn how to play golf in a variety of situations and different kinds of people, there is a limit. Why continue to play golf with people you do not like? Maybe you do like them *off* the golf course but they drive you crazy on it. Why do that to yourself? Certainly, why continue to play sucky golf and then blame it on these people? Just do not play with them. Life is too short, and a golf round too long, to not enjoy your round because of your playing partners. You do not always have a lot of control over course conditions - the wind, your lie - but you do have quite a bit of control over who you play with. Exercise it.

You Play the Wrong Tees

There seems to be a lot of pride involved in playing off the back tees, yet little pride in playing well. Far too many golfers play blue (back) tees, when they should be playing white (middle). Even some who do play white should really be playing the red (forward) tees. Unless you are shooting around par, no set of tees is "too easy".

Playing tees that are too tough for you not only balloons your score, but it puts undue stress on your swing. Liken it to weightlifting, where lifting too heavy a weight only prevents you from properly developing your form.

Playing a golf course that is too long for you (in other words, playing tees that are too far back) can also harm your shorter game. You may never develop a proper approach game, because you are always approaching from so far back (with that dreaded three-iron of yours) that you never learn the nuances of half swings, knock down shots, pitches, and so on.

Finally, the pressure on your driving becomes so enormous, because of the vast amount of real estate you have to cover, that you never learn to develop a proper, smooth, non-panicked driving style. The need to hit a big, long, drive is immense or you are hooped on such long holes.

Play the tees that are right for you, regardless of what your mates are doing. When your game becomes rock solid, and those tees literally do become too easy, then move back.

(An interesting Post Script to this: The Swedish National Team often plays the red tees to get used, mentally, to scoring low numbers. This way, when a player is in competition and on the verge of shooting a 65, they are already so used to shooting 65 that they remain mentally strong down the stretch.)

You Don't Aim At Anything When Teeing Off

Like many of the mistakes golfers make, this one most people come by innocently. There is a tee box, with two markers, we tee up the ball, and we hit it. What were we aiming at? "The fairway" many of you will say. But that is akin to a hockey player aiming at the rink. A tennis player aiming for Arthur Ashe Stadium.

We need - our eyes, body, and mind need - something very specific to aim for in order to execute a decent shot. Do not just stand up there, acknowledge the existence of the fairway, and then make a swing. Look down the fairway. Pick a spot on the fairway that could be deemed a reasonable expectation in terms of where your ball could actually land in a good (not *best*) case scenario. Maybe there is a stripe in the fairway, or a visible dead spot in the grass, anything your mind can latch onto. Aim for that, and then make a swing with purpose. I have to admit I thought this was freaky "voo-doo" thinking when first I was taught it, until the thought hit me: it would be even freakier to hit a target *without* even aiming for it.

You Point Your Feet at the Target

I have had numerous debates with many intelligent people on this issue, and while some get it, it is amazing how many do not. If your goal is to hit the target, and you align your feet (or body) to the target, you cannot possibly hit the target. (Unless you accidentally hit it, by making a mistake that counteracted the initial mistake of aligning with your feet).

If your feet are aligned to the target, and your stance is

square as it should be, your clubface cannot possibly be aligned to the target too. Correct? If you are right-handed, and your feet are aligned to the target, your clubface must be aiming right of the target. And where do most right-handers miss?

To the right.

I have had many, again seemingly intelligent, people make the idiotic argument that while this may be true, as the clubface is only a few feet in front of your shoes, you should only miss by a few feet to the right. Not true; I will explain why. Picture a golfer whose clubface is aimed at the target, and his stance is square. Perfect. Now, if he were to align his feet - rather than the clubface - to the target, he would have to rotate his body and stance several degrees to the right. He cannot simply move back or forward a few feet, because he would then have to move the ball and you are not allowed to do that the last time I checked.

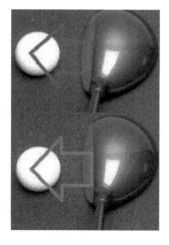

**TOP picture:
using feet to align;**

**BOTTOM picture:
using clubface to align.**

The further the ball travels in the direction of the red arrow, the further off course it gets.

Rotating your stance a few degrees in order to align your feet to the target means you are also rotating your clubface a few degrees to the right. This will send the ball on a diagonal line right of target. And because the line of the ensuing flight path is now off-target, the further the ball travels on that line, the further right of target it will go. A 200 yard shot will stray much further right of target than a 40 yard shot. Conceivably, dozens of yards. Certainly *not* a couple of feet.

Finally, the question is begged, why would you aim with your feet in the first place? Are you Maxwell Smart? Is the ball going to shoot out of your Footjoys? (I am going to see how many times I can mention Footjoy in this book; maybe they will give me some money.) Are you going to kick the ball? No. So why aim with your feet? Would they teach that at gun club? "Forget about the rifle, aim your left earlobe at the target." I do not think so. Yet another case where all logic departs for the singular reason that it is golf.

You Don't Watch Where the Ball Went

Not watching where the ball went is a natural mistake many players make, and is easy to correct. Once corrected, it will prove to be a permanent improvement in your game and golf score. When you hit the ball, watch where the darned thing goes!

It sounds obvious, but I swear to you a great many

players take their eye off the ball before it even lands. Even more watch it land but stop looking before it has finished rolling. This is why even shots that were presumed to be safe or in the fairway go inexplicably missing.

Even the shots you would think a player would watch the closest, the ones headed toward trouble, are often not watched. Take my buddy, Bogart (no please, do take him), who hits a snap hook toward the forest aside the 18th (when he is playing the 7th) and the ball is in obvious danger of never being found. By anyone. Ever. Where does Bogart look? The sky. He drops his club and looks skyward in disbelief at his poor swing. He curses the golf gods, but has no clue where his ball is actually going. The bad shot made it likely he would lose his ball; not even watching guaranteed it.

Here is an important tip: watch your ball until it rolls to a rest, then search out a nearby landmark: could be a bush, a tree, a particular fence post, a 150-yard marker, anything. Choose something distinctive so that when you get down the fairway you have a clear and identifiable reference near which you can begin your search. And yes, watch closely even when the ball is in the fairway. Many "safe" shots are not found simply because the player, using no visual reference, walked 240 yards when the ball was at the 200 yard mark.

Tour Pros have a huge advantage over recreational golfers in that they have, oh, a few thousand spectators watching their ball for them. This is not to mention the tournament marshals who are positioned purposely to see where shots go. You do not have that. Not your fault, you just do not have that luxury and need to watch the ball all the way to rest, or pay the penalty. It is hard enough to score well in golf without taking completely unnecessary penalties.

You Don't Walk Directly To Your Ball

My late, great, Dad taught me this one when I was a kid, probably because he got tired of always looking for my ball. After hitting, say, a tee shot, and your whole group has finished teeing, make a bee-line to your ball. (This is assuming you've read: "You Don't Pay Attention to Where The Ball Went"). If your ball is on the left side of the fairway, do not walk down the middle of the fairway and then turn left when you think you are equidistant to it. Walk on a diagonal line from the tee box directly to where you believe your ball to be. This way, if you incorrectly estimated the distance (Bogart always does) you are bound to come across your ball regardless.

Also, if your ball went further than you thought and into trouble, this bee-line will give you a good approximation of where the ball entered said trouble.

(One of the inherent problems of playing golf in a cart, unless you are solo in that cart, is you are not always able to make this bee-line to the ball. Often one player is on the left side, the other on the right side, making it far more difficult for the second player to find his or her ball once disoriented by the first.)

Two golfers are sitting in the clubhouse discussing their games when one says to the other,
"My game is so bad this year I had to have my ball retriever re-gripped !"

Equipment

You Use Crap Balls When Hitting Over Water

I used to tease the heck out of my Dad for this. But, he did it anyway. Parents never listen.

My Dad would get to a water hole, a hole where the shot needed to carry a pond or a creek, into his bag he would go and out would come the oldest, yellowest, and flakiest golf ball you could ever imagine. The only way it could be older is if it were made of feathers and mud.

"Why're you hittin' that, Pop?" He hated it when I called him Pop.

"Because I have to go over that water," he would say, as if we had never had this same conversation before.

"So?" I would say, as if we had never had this same conversation before.

"Well, I don't want to lose a good ball," he would explain.

There are not one, but two problems with this kind of thinking:

1. A piece of crap ball has *far* less chance of flying far enough to carry any water hazard that presents a challenge; and,
2. Psychologically you are already conceding defeat, making defeat likely.

For the answer to this dilemma, read the chapter entitled "You Don't Play With One Consistent Golf Ball."

You Don't Play With One Consistent Golf Ball

We can debate the merits of the huge variety of golf balls on the market until the cows come home. And here is not the place. But I will say this: in a game where everyone craves consistency, it makes no sense to play a variety of *different* golf balls during a round. Be it hard or soft, solid or multi-layered, cheap or expensive, you cannot be expected to know your yardages, your carries, the speed of your putts, if you are playing a Spalding one minute and a Pro V the next.

Choose a golf ball you can live with. That usually means availability and budget. Then only play that golf ball. Imagine really knowing how far a shot will go because it is with the ball *you always use*. Imagine knowing what a putt is going to feel like each and every time, because you are using the same brand *and type* of golf ball you are used to. Imagine knowing which ball in the fairway is yours and when asked, not struggling to remember, "Was I playing a Top-Flite x-out? Or was it a Canada Cup?"

It is a simple thing, and does not require one extra minute of practice. Choose a golf ball and go with it. If you decide a month down the road you do not like that golf ball, that is a good thing. Stop using it, never use it again, choose another ball, and go with it.

Your Golf Bag Is Too Heavy

I have done my stint working in golf club pro shops, and over the years picked up a great many golf bags. Many, of those great many, were very, very heavy.

Loaded with everything from bowling balls to the

kitchen sink, some of these golf bags weighed up to fifty pounds. Funnier yet, some of the owners of these weighty pieces would fight each other to get the smoothest rolling pull cart. I guess so!

Golf balls were the biggest culprit in weighing these bags down. It was not uncommon for a heavy golf bag to contain upwards of thirty golf balls. No one needs thirty golf balls. Not in their bag for one round, anyway.

Pulling or carrying a heavy golf bag is taxing, no matter who you are, and energy conserved is energy available for those key holes late in the round. Go through your golf bag and take an inventory. Do you really need everything in there? Do you need two rain suits? Do you even need one today? Have you ever lost more than eight golf balls in a round? If yes, then leave as many in there as you think you might need, even add one more, but draw the line. Put the rest in a box in the trunk of your car. Lighten your load, and lower your score.

You Don't Have a Sand Wedge

Now this is not entirely your fault, especially if you are a beginner, as most (nearly all) golf sets do not come with a sand wedge. Oddly, many come with a 3-iron which you probably have no business hitting, but not a sand wedge.

You cannot play a decent round of golf without packing a sand wedge. I told Bogart this and now he never plays without a ham and cheese. But I digress. Why do you need a sand wedge? Sand traps, that's why. They are everywhere! And at some point you are going to need to get out of them, and believe me a pitching wedge will not do. A pitching wedge does not have the flange, the bounce, or the loft to make getting out of a sand trap easy. Each time you enter a sand trap wielding a pitching wedge you are probably adding a good half a shot, to a shot, to your score on average. And even if you were lucky enough to get out of the trap you are probably not going to get as close to the hole as you would with a sand wedge.

Furthermore, sand wedges are very useful around the green for chipping. That's right; they are not just for sand. They are especially good for short approach shots as they hit the ball higher, make it spin more, and give you a greater chance of holding the green should you accidentally hit it.

You Don't Have a Lob Wedge

If you are really serious about improving your score, a lob wedge is a must purchase. Also known generically as a 60 degree wedge it gives you four more degrees of loft than a sand wedge. A lob wedge is extremely useful around the green for chipping, and for short approach shots where you might have to make a baby or half swing with a pitching wedge. Instead, you can make a relatively full swing with a lob wedge. A lob wedge does not have to be expensive, but it does have to be purchased. Sell your one iron and buy a lob wedge today.

You Do Have a 3 Iron

I am sorry, but a three-iron is an antiquated piece of metal that does not belong in most recreational golfers' bags. The shaft is long, the head is small, the loft minimal, the swing weight awkward. There are so many wonderful and varied hybrids and fairway woods on the market today that it does not make sense to even carry the *weight* of a three-iron, let alone attempt to use one and increase your chances of a poor shot, or worse. And that is all I really have to say about that. Except that three-irons can be useful tree stakes.

Your Shafts Are Too Stiff

I would say for every player who plays tees that are too tough for them, there is another player (perhaps even the same player) who plays with clubs that are too stiff for them.

This next statement is important to grasp: Bubba Watson plays with regular shafts. Relatively. He swings *so fast* that his shafts bend with the same degree of whippiness as Bogart playing senior shafts. The degree of whip in your shafts should relate to your swing speed, not your strength. An ox with a slow swing should play whippy shafts. And take extra care to repair his spike marks.

I blame sales people for golfers who play with stiff shafts when they should not be. It is a bit of a come-on in the sales process to tell the customer how big and strong he is, and that he should play with shafts stiffer than rebar. And remember, sales people are far more interested in getting rid of excess stock sitting in the back than truly fitting you to the right clubs. Many years in pro shops taught me that. So, yes, sales people are partly to blame for why you suck at golf.

One final note, a whippy shaft (within reason) promotes clubhead speed. Clubhead speed equals distance. 'Nuf said. (Okay I lied, one more thing: to see what shafts are right for you, visit a golf repair centre and consult an expert who is *not* interested in selling you clubs.)

You Don't Change Your Grips Often Enough

The second you begin to take your club back from address elements of chance are introduced to the game. Any element of chance we knowingly allow that precedes the swinging of the club is just plain dumb. Playing golf with less than perfect grips introduces chance before you even get out of your car.

Grips are not that expensive. Re-gripping all your irons should cost less than one round of golf. Grips are, quite literally, your connection to the golf club. A pretty important connection. Grips do not have to be "worn out" to warrant replacement. Grips age, dry, crack, become slick. If our aim is consistency, in a game where consistency is elusive, re-gripping only a portion of your clubs does not promote consistency.

Many will say you should re-grip your clubs once a year. But you and I know that is not going to happen. So let's saw off at this: don't you dare re-grip your clubs any less frequently than every other year. And if you do want to spread the cost out a little, a good plan would be to re-grip all your irons one year, all your woods the next year, alternating year to year.

(Notice how I wrote this piece without resorting to the nauseating "Get a grip!" joke? You're welcome.)

A fellow tees off and slices his ball right into the oncoming traffic of an adjacent highway, hitting a car and smashing its windshield. The driver gets out and runs up to the golfer to remonstrate with him. "You sliced your ball right into my car, what are you going to do about it?" the driver demanded to know. The golfer thought about it a minute and said, "I think I am going to have to close my stance a little."

Swing

Your Grip Is Too Strong

A good grip is what is termed a "neutral" grip. This is essentially where, making the rude assumption one is right-handed, the back of the left hand is facing down the fairway, the palm of the right hand is facing down the fairway, and the back of the right hand is facing the opposite direction to your intended target.

Many golfers have what is called a "strong" grip. This is where the back of the left hand is facing the sky, basically, and the right palm has rolled underneath the shaft, also pointing skyward. The reason this is called a strong grip is because it was thought that this hand position promoted a rolling over of the writsts during the swing, creating a hooking action. The inference being a hook is a strong shot, and a slice is a weak shot.

However, most players with a strong grip do not actually turn their wrists over. Instead, they use their hands to hit up and the result is a shot that is weak right. The whole motivation, albeit a subconscious one, for putting the right hand under the shaft is to get into a hitting up position. The right hand can flip up as the club goes under the ball. There is only one catch. You do not hit up to hit a golf shot, you hit down.

You Don't Choke Down On Your Club

Far too many (right-handed) golfers play golf with the butt of their club sticking *in* to the palm of their left hand. This causes movement of the grip within your hand which amounts to a variable we just do not need in a game we are trying to play more consistently.

And it wrecks your expensive leather glove.

Choke down on the club so that the butt end is clearly protruding from your left hand, and your left pinkie is wrapped around it. The club will remain far more still in your hand, increasing your feeling of (and actual) control when swinging.

I even recommend choking down yet another half an inch. By doing this, you turn your five-iron, for instance, into six-iron length with the benefits of five-iron loft. You will lose a *smidgen* of distance, but improved shotmaking will more than make up for that. And for real amusement, you should see Bogart choke down a hot dog!

Your Backswing is Too Big

There are three key components to a backswing:
- weight on back foot;
- clubhead higher than hands;
- back to the target.

So many players put such an emphasis on making a big backswing that they fail to achieve the above three components. And their backswing is so big, their back is not even to the target because they have over-rotated. As soon as the backswing becomes too big, and the club goes beyond horizontal at the so-called top of the backswing (in which case the clubhead is now *lower* than the hands) you now have to swing the club back *up* before you can swing it down at the ball. The swing is hard enough without having to do it in multiple directions.

Another by-product of too big a backswing, ironically, is deceleration on the downswing. The swing feels out of control and in order to theoretically gain some control, the player unwittingly slows the downswing, decelerating, causing the clubhead to veer off path. (To "hug" a path, something moving on any kind of an arc [race car, bicycle, even an acrobat or high jumper] must be *accelerating* in order to attain the benefits of centripetal force.)

You Keep Your Head Too Still

The dumbest advice ever dispensed in any sport is the one told to golfers each and every day: "Keep Your Head Still".

Ever ask, *"Why?"*

It became apparent, a long, long time ago, to some golf instructors, that poor players moved their head a lot. Instead of trying to figure out why those poor players were moving their heads so much, they decided instead to say, "Don't do that. Keep your head still." Ahhh, if it were only that easy.

Golfers who hit up at the ball display a lot of head movement. The physical act of the body hitting up, drives the head up. On the flipside, golfers who hit down have much less head movement. It makes more sense to teach a player to hit down, than to tell them to make an athletic action while keeping their head still. I cannot think of another athletic endeavour in the world where that kind of direction would be made, and it should not happen in golf either.

The player who arbitrarily tries to keep their head perfectly still, while swinging a golf club, gets very stiff, very cautious, has no weight shift, reverse pivots, cannot complete a backswing, cannot swing down aggressively, and has trouble releasing the golf club. And I have not even touched on the bad stuff. If anyone ever tells you to keep your head still, smack theirs.

You Don't Hit Down, Dammit!

"Reverse every natural instinct and do the opposite of what you are inclined to do, and you will probably come very close to having a perfect golf swing."
Ben Hogan

Nothing could be truer when it comes to what is required to get a golf ball in the air. Despite the fact the ball is below us, and usually on the ground, sometimes even in deep grass, our natural instinct is to hit up at it to get it airborne. Hit up at something that is below us, with its underside virtually inaccessible. Ah but this is golf, logic goes out the window, right?

Wrong.

The only way to get a golf ball consistently up in the air is to *hit down* at it with a specially manufactured tool designed for the job. Your golf club.

While on the surface one might think that hitting down at something on the ground might drive it into the ground, note the shape and design of a golf clubhead. It is ill-suited to driving things into the ground. Due to the loft of the clubface, any attempt to drive a ball into the ground results in the ball compressing, then spinning – backwards - up and off the clubface. We have elevation, and we have backspin, two of the holy grails of golf. Now if Bogart would just stop wearing lycra.

An American golfer has the rare treat of playing the Old Course at St. Andrews, with a caddy no less. Part way through the round he asks his caddy if he has noticed any reason for his bad tee shots, to which the caddy replies, "Aye, there's a piece of shit on the end of your driver." The Golfer picks up his driver and cleans the club face, at which point the caddy says, "No, the other end!"

Practice

You Tinker With Your Swing

I have never seen a "tinkerer" who I could call a really good player. Why? Because they never have "a" swing long enough to get good at it. It never gets a chance to "set".

If you do not know what you are doing while tinkering, you do not know what you are disturbing as opposed to fixing. I equate it to me tinkering under the hood of my car (which would be a *bad* idea) and accidentally breaking something without realizing it, and never fixing whatever may have needed fixing. Now I have two things broken. It is worse with a golf swing. The tinkerer golfer who now has *two* swing flaws - thanks to his tinkering – will, and almost has to, make swing compensations just to get through a round. Now they have *three* flaws. Or maybe more?

Stop tinkering. Get lessons, and/or practice sensibly and get good at the swing you do have. But do not tinker.

You Don't Practice With a Plan

Very few sports demand practice to succeed as much as golf. Very few sportspeople practice as haphazardly as golfers.

Your game will improve as the quality of your practice improves. Your practice will only improve when you start practicing with a plan. I do not even really mind what your plan is, as long as you have one. You are smarter than Bogart, you can write down a plan that is not pointless. The very act of making the plan makes you accountable, whereas it really is easy to "practice stupid" if you just show up, dump out a bucket of balls, and start hitting.

You Don't Target Practice

There is a widespread notion among many golfers that they hit the ball beautifully at the range, but everything falls to pieces on the golf course. There may be a smidgen of truth to this, but usually in these situations there is simply a "mis-appraisal" of how well the golfer was actually doing at the range. This is because, in far too many cases, the barometer for success is off as there is no target involved. I would have aced many of my exams in high school if the teachers did not insist on grading the papers.

Bogart stands at the range, dumps out his jumbo double extra large caramel bucket of balls with no fat, and wails away. The range is huge, and he makes good use of the square footage. Shots all over the place. But boy does his swing feel good. He then takes, as Moe Norman used to call it, "the longest walk in golf". The walk from the range to the first tee. Suddenly the fairway is narrow, nets are replaced by trees, and there's all these wet and sandy areas. Just as suddenly his collar tightens as if badly laundered. The backswing gets cautious; you can almost hear the downswing squeak, and bam. Wait, no bam, he missed.

Without adding a single minute of practice your game could improve simply by choosing a very real target for every single shot you do hit at the range. I will finish with this: I once had a student tell me she had gone to the range the night before and her seven-iron was not very consistent. I asked what she was aiming at.

"Nothing," she replied.

"Then how do you know?" I inquired.

You Don't Mix It Up When You Practice

Rarely do we hit twenty five-irons in a row in a golf game. And if you do, you really do suck.

In practice it is not uncommon at all, nor is it inadvisable, to hit twenty or more of the same club in a row. That repetition is a key part of training and developing muscle memory.

However, you must dedicate a portion of your practice time to what I call "mixing it up". Better said: replicating a game situation during your practice session. Hit a driver, put it back in the bag, take out a five-iron and hit that, followed by a wedge, and then even a chip. Repeat this (or similar) for a good ten to twenty minutes per practice session.

If you have hit nineteen drivers in a row the twentieth should be easy. To hit just one, and well, on demand and under the pressure of a game situation? Another thing entirely, so you must practice that scenario too.

You Don't Practice Half-Wedges

For some bizarre reason, it seems a bucket of balls is

not worth the money you paid for it unless each ball hit goes a long way.

Bogart will bang out fifty shots, 200 yards each, and feel he got his money's worth out of a bucket of balls. Suggest he hit some 25-yard half wedges? "That's a waste of money!" he says.

No it is not.

Not only will you have to hit *plenty* of half-wedges in a golf game, but it is vital to remember what a half-wedge is scored as in a game: *one stroke*. How many of you have ever played a par five beautifully for the first two shots, leaving yourself a half-wedge in, botched the half-wedge and gone on to make double bogey? We all have.

Practicing half-wedges is crucial to your success, not only to avoid hitting half-wedges that suck, but because it is really beneficial that they be somewhat accurate. You can bomb a drive and be happy with the result either side of the fairway. But a half-wedge to the wrong side of the green? Probably another wasted shot.

While some do not practice half-wedges because they do not realize their importance, many do not practice them because they are simply not good at them. It is demoralizing to hit such a small shot, poorly. But guess what? You will eventually get good at half-wedges. If you practice them!

You Don't Practice After You Play

I do not practice after I play, so I do not mean to sound a hypocrite here. But I would be a better player if I did.

Tour Pros practice after their round, and it makes total sense. It is not unusual to have a slight bug in your swing during a round, but during the round is not the time to fix it. If you are a working stiff like most of us, your next opportunity to work out that bug – other than right after your round – may be days or even a week away. By then you may not be able to consciously remember, let alone recall the physical feel of, what was going on with your swing during your last round.

Granted, it is their day job, but a Tour Pro almost immediately hits the range after their round to hit balls while everything is fresh in their mind and body. We could too. After all, the range is right there; we do not even have to get in the car or put our shoes on.

The only reason I play golf is to bug my wife. She thinks I'm having fun.

Short Game

You Don't Have a Chipping Strategy

What makes chipping difficult is virtually no two chip shots are alike. Your ball could be in the exact same position by the green on Tuesday as Monday, but, the flag is not. Completely different chip shot required.

Feel is beneficial in chipping, but it is not the nucleus. A good chipping strategy is. And, the good news? There is only one chipping strategy you need to learn. You can stray from it, and it is entirely your call when to stray from it, but you cannot stray from it if you do not know it in the first place.

There are few absolutes and constants in chipping, but there are two you can take to the bank:

1. No matter where you are there is always a portion of the green that is closer to you than the rest of the green; and,
2. More often than not a rolling golf ball is easier to predict than a flying one.

For the purposes of this strategy we are going to call the portion of the green closest to you "the front of the green". Even if you are behind the green, from where you are standing now the "front of the green" is the portion that is nearest. A very sound, tried, and true strategy is to chip the ball from where you are, to the front of the green, and let it roll the rest of the way to the hole. You can control the amount the ball rolls after landing quite simply: with club choice. Want a lot of roll? Chip with a five-iron. Want little roll? Chip with a lob wedge. Always the same swing, always the same target (front of the green), <u>not</u> always the same club. (Always chipping with a pitching wedge is tantamount to always eating food with a fork. You should see Bogart eating tomato soup with a fork!)

One time out of ten this strategy may need to be broken. You are intelligent; armed with the knowledge of the strategy, you can figure out when to depart from it. But, you know what? Even if you *never* strayed from the strategy and it backfired a couple of times, the *overall* improvement would be so drastic it would more than make up for the odd failure.

You Only Chip With One Club

It is a very misguided notion that pitching wedges are for chipping. It is not called a *chipping* wedge. As no two chip shots are alike, you cannot expect one club to tackle an infinite number of scenarios.

A good chip shot hits the green early, and rolls the rest of the way to the hole. If you have a lot of stuff to get over before the ball reaches the green, you may need a high lofted club (higher than a pitching wedge, even). If there is little terrain to get over, a lower lofted club will do. If you do not want the ball to roll very far after landing on the green, a higher lofted club is preferable. If you need the ball to roll a long way, as low lofted a club as possible is required.

As you were reading the above you may have been asking, "ya but what if....?" Precisely. What if you have a lot to get over *and* you need the ball to roll a long way? What if you are very close to the green but do not want the ball to roll far? The answer: it is a good thing we have fourteen clubs in our bag to choose from, and we are not just limiting ourselves to the good ol' pitching wedge.

You Worry More About Line Than Speed When Putting

There are two key elements to putting, and they are not

equal. Unfortunately most struggling golfers focus on the element that is less equal. The two elements are:
a) line; and,
 b) speed.

Most golfers offer more attention to line than they do speed, and it should be the other way around. Why? Simply because there is a greater variable in speed than there is in line.

Bogart has a twenty foot putt. (His putt does look big in those pants.) He lines it up, and strokes the ball with his putter. Which of the following is more likely?

- he hits it ten feet long or short of the hole;
- he hits it ten feet right or left of the hole.

The chances of missing a putt by ten entire feet to the right or left are slim, even with a breaking putt. But to leave a twenty foot putt ten feet short? Eminently do-able. Run it past by ten feet? Could happen easily. *Especially* if you were not paying attention to speed in the first place, and more worried about plumb-bobbing.

When you putt, gauging the speed of the putt (essentially the distance) should be your number one priority. If you get your speed right, and are off line by an entire two feet, what do you have left? That's right, a two-foot putt. Get your line right to within six inches, but knock it ten feet by? You have a testy ten-foot come-backer to deal with, and your work may be far from over.

Unless you are absolutely blind your intuitive sense of line will be reasonable. Make the speed the priority. And if both line and speed happen to be good, you may even start sinking some long ones!

You Don't Examine a Putt from Both Sides of the Hole

It takes about thirty extra seconds. If you do it as a matter of course, it can take no extra time. Do not just judge a putt from where the ball is. Walk around to the opposite side of the hole and examine your putt from there. You will see wondrous and varied things, I promise you. You will see breaks you never saw before, you will notice changes in grade, more (or less) severe than first thought, you may even see the crow that was about to take your sandwich off your pull cart.

If you make a habit of always examining both sides of a putt, you will also develop ways of saving time. For instance, if my ball is below the hole, I will go and drop my clubs off at the back of the green, above the hole. As I walk from my clubs to the ball I make note of what my putt looks like from this side, so when I get to the ball my homework is already done.

"Your trouble is that you're not addressing the ball correctly."
"Yeah, well I've been polite to the bloody thing for long enough."

Behaviour

You Drink On the Golf Course

What I am about to say here has nothing to do with morals. It is about golf. It is about why you suck at golf. You drink on the golf course.

It is extremely well documented that alcohol in your system negatively affects your coordination, your reaction time, and your mental judgement. It is illegal to drive a vehicle while under the influence of alcohol for these very reasons. It is harder to drive a golf ball than it is to drive a car. Not more dangerous, but more difficult.

There are extremely few sports where drinking a beer is an integral part of playing the game. Fewer still that have a cart come up to you mid-session and sell you the stuff. I have played hockey with some of the biggest booze hounds this side of Mystery, Alaska, and even they wait until they hit the dressing room *after* the game to start drinking.

I enjoy a beer as much as Bogart does, so again, this is not a moral issue. It is a 'do you want to play good golf' issue. If you truly want to be sharp and play the game decently, drink after your game. While you collect your bets. They even have an extra hole expressly for this purpose, called the 19th hole. If you do not care how you play the game then go ahead and get hammered. But, if you want to play well… I'm just sayin'…

You Don't Know Your Yardages

One (of many) advantages Tour Professionals have over recreational golfers does not have to do with talent, but information. Those players know, within a yard, exactly how far each and every club will go in normal conditions. (Knowing this means too that they can make adjustments in abnormal conditions.)

This does not mean, however, that the recreational golfer cannot benefit from the same sort of information. Figuring out how far each club goes is not that difficult. It just takes the realization that you ought to figure this out if you want to stop flying over greens or coming up short, and then paying careful attention to how far your shots actually are going both in play, and in practice.

Bogart will miss a green ten yards short and then throw his club. A good player will make note of where they are standing in relation to the green (100 yards out? 150 yards out?) and then consider the club they just hit. When they get to the ball they will pace off exactly how short they were. You are 150 yards out, you hit an eight-iron, you came up ten yards short. If this happens a lot, it is safe to say your eight-iron goes approximately 140 yards on average. So, next time you will want to try a seven-iron. You keep doing this until you become very familiar with your average yardages.

(Tip: Most full sized, non-beginning golfers should see about ten yards' incremental difference between each club. Therefore you do not have to memorize the distance of every club, just one or two benchmark clubs. I always remember I hit my seven-iron, safely and on average, 150 yards. Remembering this, all I need is math to figure out the others (eight-iron: 140 yards, six-iron: 160 yards, and so on.)

You Don't Pace Off Your Shots

Knowing how far you hit a club does not help if you do not know how far you need to hit one. This is another advantage of the Tour Professional, who on every shot has an employee telling them how far they have to the green, to a bunker, to a water crossing, to the bar.

Short of going out and buying an expensive GPS range finder, all you have to do on a given shot is locate something that gives you a yardage reference. That could be a 150 yard marker at the side of the fairway, a 100 yard plate in the middle of the fairway, or, especially useful, a sprinkler head in the fairway with the exact yardage from the head to the green marked right on it.

There is a good chance that what you find will not be equidistant to where you are, so you will need to pace off the distance from the marker to your location. Do this by taking long strides, hopefully approximating one yard per stride, from the marker to your ball. If the marker is on the right side of the fairway and your ball on the left side, do *not* do this diagonally as it will throw off the true yardage. Pace down the right side until you appear to be equal with your ball. Oh, and do not pull a Bogart and forget to *count* your paces! You need to know how many, so you can add or subtract from the yardage of the marker to determine how far from the green you are.

You Focus Too Much On Hitting Greens in Regulation

Hitting greens in regulation (landing on the green in

one shot on a par three, in two on a par four, in three on a par five) is:

too much pressure;

unrealistic pressure.

The notion that very good golfers hit virtually all eighteen greens in regulation is a completely false one. At the 2003 Masters, one of the competitors hit just 52% of the greens, in regulation, throughout the four rounds of competition. You would expect a pro, let alone one who qualified for The Masters, to do better than that you might think. He did not have to. His name was Mike Weir; he won the championship.

A 100+ shooter could improve their game to the high eighties without ever hitting a green in regulation. An eighties shooter could move into the seventies hitting just five greens.

One of the reasons focusing on greens in regulation is detrimental to the average player's game is the effect it has on club choice. Example: long par four, and Bogart pulls out his three-wood for the second shot, "Why the three-wood?" I ask him.

"Well," he says in a tone that already intimates my question has an obvious answer, "I'm over 200 yards away; I'll never get there with anything else."

Never is a strong word, and inaccurate. He could hit five wedges and eventually get there, so "never" does not apply. The real question is: while he could conceivably get there with a three-wood, what are the chances? In Bogart's case, one in ten, and I am being kind.

The even bigger question is: what are the repercussions if he hits the three-wood poorly? And, sure enough, he hit it out of bounds. Add a couple to his score, and we are not even in the hole yet. Two seven-irons, or a five and a nine, should have had him on in three, and putting for par, bogey at worst. Bogart shoots in the mid to high nineties, so eighteen bogeys would see him on the cusp of breaking ninety. If only he played smart golf.

The cold hard truth is, and I cannot apologize for this because it needs to be said, *most* recreational golfers have no business trying to hit every green in regulation, and would *lower their scores* if they stopped trying.

Finally, do not get me wrong; if you hit a great drive and reaching the green with your next shot is within you, I am not suggesting you deliberately miss. But I am saying the notion that good golf = lots of greens in regulation is complete and utter bunk. Mike Weir has a green jacket to prove it.

You Don't Know When to Lay Up

More golf tournaments have been won with a lay-up than a miracle shot. It is just that no one is clamouring to fill television highlight reels with lay-ups, naturally, so they are not as well documented.

A good player knows when to lay up. A good lay-up

requires patience, knowledge, good club selection, and accurate shotmaking. It is not a cop out. In fact, it takes a lot of confidence to say, "I am going to lay up to 100 yards out and then stick the approach."

A good lay-up can:

- avoid a costly water hazard completely;
- put two easy clubs in your hands instead of one impossible one;
- put you at a favourite yardage from which you historically perform well.

It is a well known adage in sports to play to your strengths and avoid your weaknesses. Why so many golfers insist on doing it the other way around is a mystery.

You Try To Work the Ball

I once played a round of golf with a young apprentice professional from my club. Before we started out he was telling me of his goal of not just being a club professional, but of playing on the big tours. In his estimation, his only shortcoming was the fact he could only hit the ball straight. He felt that in order to make it to the top level he would need to learn to work the ball.

I was quite excited about the forthcoming round

because I had never played with someone who could only hit the ball straight. In fact, I had never even known of anyone who could only hit the ball straight, except perhaps for childhood hero Moe Norman. And by the conclusion of the round with this young man, I had still never played with anyone who could only hit the ball straight. Unless you count "straight into the trees".

You would think that most golfers would love to hit the ball straight, even if *only* straight. Yet I am constantly surprised at the number of golfers, most of whom cannot break 100, who think they need to know how to "bend the ball"; that fading, drawing, slicing and hooking - on demand - are vital assets to a good game. I always counter that just learning to hit the ball straight, and straight only, is challenge enough, and if even mildly accomplished it will do far more for your game than "working" the ball. And I will share with you a very common reaction, and you tell me what you would say to a fellow who says the following: "But what if you are in the right trees and need to hit a slice to get out of the trees and to the green?" What would you say to this fellow? Probably, hopefully, the same thing I say, "If you hit the ball straight you wouldn't be in the right trees in the first place!"

Working on hitting the ball straight – *only* - has a double-benefit. One, the obvious, that you will hit more fairways, and more greens. The other, that working on this will mean you have one swing to work on and memorize, whereas trying to shape a variety of shots means potential confusion to your swing muscle memory. Remember, too, that it is harder to judge the potential result of a curving shot, whereas it is much easier to predict the result of a straight shot. Straight is straight, whereas a slice can vary in shape and distance dramatically. So, you could end up hitting that slice out of the trees you wanted, only to see it slice right back into the trees again. Work on hitting the ball straight and when that gets boring, call me.

You Talk Too Much

Some people just do not shut up on the golf course. They talk on the tee, they talk on the fairway, they talk on the green, they talk, talk, talk. It is very annoying to other golfers on the course, and especially to playing partners whose games it can distract. But... it ain't too good for the game of the guy who is doing the yacking, either.

Someone who is incessantly talking cannot possibly be concentrating on their overall game, let alone the shot pending. Golf is a social game, I get that. But you do not have to talk for four straight hours in order to be sociable. Know when to talk, when to stop, even what to talk about. Do not start a story that cannot be completed in the couple of minutes it takes for you walk up the fairway. Switch it off a good minute before you have to prepare for your next shot, and then focus. Get dialed in to what is required: where is your ball in relation to the hole, what is the wind doing, where are any hazards you need to be aware of, what club do you think you might hit? You cannot consider any of these things properly if you are yacking away. And the aforementioned are *all* things that can affect your game without changing a single swing nuance or muscle in your body.

You Don't Talk Enough

"I don't what?" you're asking me. But for every two golfers who talk too much on the golf course, there is one golfer who does not talk enough for their own good.

Who I am talking about is the "intense" player. This is the player who knows you need to concentrate to play golf, but does not know you cannot possibly "concentrate" for four hours uninterrupted. They are the ones who walk down the right side of the fairway when everyone else is walking down the left. They are constantly thinking about their game, their swing mechanics, the upcoming shot, and do not want any of this intense concentration interrupted by idle chit chat.

Watch the pros on TV. Television coverage does not do this enough, but when they do show a couple of players walking down the fairway they are often "chit-chatting" about something. Might be the football score from the night before, someone cute they saw in the gallery, something. They know they have to break up the intensity so they do not wear themselves out just concentrating! However, they know when to switch it off, also, and focus on the next shot. You can do it too, and your game will only benefit.

You Don't Know the Rules

I never cease to be shocked at the number of players – including pros – who do not know the rules, or do not know to, or how to, look them up in game situations.

Many a player takes penalties where they could be avoided, takes the wrong number of strokes as penalty, or plays shots in situations from which they are entitled to relief. The rules can work against you, of course, but they can also work for you. They cannot work for you, however, if you do not know the rules of golf.

Here is a perhaps obscure, yet classic example of a player knowing the rules, and legitimately making them work for him in a tournament situation. I am not talking about the Tiger Woods boulder-moving incident, but really that is a good example, too. No, this was Bernhard Langer, a great many years ago. His golf ball was between a cart path and some bushes. It was not touching the cart path and was quite close to the bushes. In fact it was so close to the bushes that he could not take a proper stance if he played the shot his natural hand, right-handed. So, he decided to play the shot left-handed, which is his right. Or is it left? Anyway, to play the shot left-handed he would have to stand on the cart path. He argued, successfully, that as he would have to stand on the cart path he was entitled to relief. And, he got it. Once relief was taken, he now had room to hit the ball right-handed. Which he did. Remember, the rules will screw you if you let them, so know them well and you can get some shots back.

You Spend Too Much Time Scrounging for Balls

Golf balls are not cheap, granted, and if you stumble upon a nice Titleist (Titleist owns Footjoy by the way) and it is not still rolling, by all means pick it up. But, I have *never* seen a good player that jumps at every opportunity to dive into the woods to search for lost golf balls. It is time consuming and diverts your focus away from the game at hand - the game you do not want to suck at.

If you know where there is a gold mine of golf balls, go there another time and fill your boots. Or, go to Walmart, or patronize the little kid on the corner selling golf balls in egg cartons. But, when you are on the golf course, playing a game, counting your strokes, stop scrounging and perhaps you will not need so many balls in the first place.

You Swing Harder With Your Long Clubs

Don't deny it, you do it. You swing your wedge

normally, but when you bring out a longer club, like your driver, you try to smack the crap out of it. This begs the following questions:

1. Why do you hit a driver?
2. Why do you try to kill said driver?
3. Why do you not realize that the answer to #1 above overrides the answer to #2?

The answer to #1 is both obvious, and reasonable. You hit a driver for one reason, and one reason only: for distance. Fair enough. When swung properly the driver hits the ball further than any other club in your bag. *When swung properly.* If you already have more ammunition in your hands, why the need to swing harder? It is like getting into a race car and hitting the accelerator harder than a regular car. In second gear. It is a race car! It already goes faster, you do not need to stomp on the accelerator. All that does is create a lot of noise and smoke, like Bogart's last barbecue.

You need one swing. You want one swing. It is easier to learn one swing (you're getting sleeeepy). It is easier to perfect one swing. You have thirteen clubs you can use with that one swing. One swing = thirteen different yet predictable results. Multiple swings (and/or multiple intensities of swing) with thirteen different clubs = an infinite number of ways to screw up your golf game.

You Hit Your Driver Too Often

Nowhere in the rule book does it say you must hit a driver off the tee on all par fours and par fives.

Nowhere. I checked.

The player who limits themselves to hitting just one club from nearly all tees is akin to the player who only chips with a pitching wedge. With so many clubs at your disposal, why limit yourself to just one tool for a given task?

The answer I get usually is, "But don't you want to hit it a long way?" Sure, that would be nice, but you do not want to hit it into trouble, either. I am not just talking about the risk of a poor shot with golf's most difficult club. Lots of golf courses have holes designed to snare driver hitters. For instance, why hit a driver on a hole where there happens to be a fairway bunker right smack dab at the distance you usually hit your driver? Why hit a driver on a dogleg you might hit through? Why hit a driver on a dogleg that bends the opposite way to the natural flight of your drives?

I am not saying give up your driver completely; it is a club in your bag and deserves to be used. I am saying, be creative. Think of alternatives. Play smart. Know your talents. Then, when confronted with a super wide par five fairway, wail away!

You Don't Have A Pre-Shot Routine

Bogart's pre-shot routine consists of praying, but you can do better than that.

The very best players in the world *all* have a consistent pre-shot routine. Even when Sergio went through his phase of incessantly gripping and re-gripping the club at address, he always did it seventeen times. That is too many times, obviously, but it was never sixteen and never eighteen. (One could argue his game did not improve at all after he felt pressured to limit this unusual pre-shot behaviour.)

The point is, if you want consistency, you have to go about things in a consistent manner. A consistent pre-shot routine not only fosters the obvious, consistency, but it calms the mind. Any thoughts of "Oh I really need this shot" or "boy that pond looks big. Hey, was that an alligator?" are quelled once you enter into your habitual pre-shot routine. The mind clicks into the routine, and then the ensuing learned mechanics of the swing engage, greatly increasing your chances of a good shot.

You Stray From Your Routine Under Pressure

The point of a pre-shot routine lies in the word "routine". The point is to do it the same way *all of the time*. Not most of the time. The worst thing you can do when finding yourself under pressure is to abandon, or change, your routine.

The most common mistake under pressure is one of

adding extra, unnecessary, practice swings. Under pressure, even players who do not normally take practice swings start taking them like Bogart takes spring rolls at a Chinese buffet. What is pressure in golf? It is generally pressure we place on ourselves. It seems to be at its greatest, ironically, when we are playing well.

You know the scenario: Bogart is playing the round of his life. Two holes left. Par in and he has a career best. Suddenly, the practice swings start coming in buckets. Three practice swings, four practice swings, five. Geese change directions due to the resultant wind. If this is you, think about this: you have been playing well! You would not be in this situation if you had not been. Do what you have been doing all day; do not change now. If you were taking one practice swing on holes one through sixteen, take one practice swing now. And shoot. It is not a guarantee of a great shot, but it does heighten your chances of success.

You Attempt Miracle Shots When You're Not Playing Well

This is a classic symptom of a poor golfer, although it is also something easy to sympathize with.
Bogart is playing poorly; very poorly. His swing is just not clicking and his score is escalating like a taxi meter in Manhattan at rush hour. Par five. Drive in the trees and no choice but to punch out. He is in the fairway

now but flubs his third shot. Out comes the driver.

What?

The thinking is a miracle driver off the deck could get him on the green and perhaps salvage a bogey or even par. There is only one problem. He is not swinging well! His drive went into the trees and a routine iron from the fairway went ten feet. On what information is he basing the decision to hit the most difficult club in the bag straight off the short stuff?

His decision is motivated by desperation, not information, and it is just plain dumb. It sucks to play poorly. We have all done it. But know when you are playing poorly, muddle through it as best you can (go to the range straight after your round) and live to fight another day. Do not attempt shots that are high risk on a good day, when you are playing badly today. It only makes the bleeding worse.

You Complain About Score, But Are More Worried About Ball Striking

For the average golfer their satisfaction with the game can be measured in one of two ways: score, or ball striking.

Part of the allure of golf is the feel of that perfect shot. You know the feeling, you have hit one or two. Effortless, poetry in motion, the ball just flies off the clubface. Even if you only hit a few of them, just two or three are enough to keep us coming back. I call it the nicotine shot in golf.

However, constantly striving for that perfect shot can get in the way of playing good golf. You need to make a decision. Do you care about your score, or how the shots feel? If you truly care about how the shots feel, fine. Go for it. But, do not complain about your score at the same time.

Golf is a game where the objective is to get the ball in the hole in as few shots as possible. It really does not matter how the shots feel in doing it. A baseball player who hits a bloop single does not concern himself with the fact the ball coming off the bat did not feel like down on a goose. The hockey player who deflects someone else's shot into the net with the shank of his stick does not go home wishing that game winning goal felt better. The tennis player who won Wimbledon with a mis-hit that just dribbled over the net is doing just fine, thank you very much. If you care about your score, stop worrying about how the shots feel, and start working on the scoring part of the game.

And we can all learn from this: the great ball striker *Ben Hogan* once said he figured about four shots in an average round actually felt good. The rest he just hoped went in the right direction.

You're Too Emotional

Golfers can be emotional people. Many, seemingly not

emotional in their day to day lives, can cry like babies on the golf course. Many, seemingly without temper in their day to day lives, can throw a club 50 yards in a fit of fury. Let's not even start with the people who *are* emotional in their day to day lives. Poor Bogart.

Part of what makes golf unique is that emotion is so prevalent and plays such a part of the outcome of the game. The thing is, in order to play really good golf, we need to set emotion aside. Quite honestly, emotion has no place in a good game of golf.

I am not sure what it is that makes golfers cling so emotionally to every shot they hit. A cricket batsmen who has a golden opportunity for a six, and misses, has forgotten about it ten minutes later. A golfer who has a golden opportunity for birdie, and ultimately bogeys, can carry the associated negative feelings around with him into next month, let alone the next hole. Forget about being grumpy with his caddy the remainder of his round, he can be grumpy with his co-workers the remainder of the week. All because of a bad putt, or a lost drive, a chunked chip, a botched sand shot. I cannot think of another sport where mistakes are so keenly remembered.

Golfers are even tough on themselves when misfortune begets success. A hockey player who accidentally scores when the puck bounces into the net off his helmet raises his stick and cheers. The golfer who shanks the ball off a tree and into the hole remembers the shank, not the outcome.

Why do we do this? Part of the reason is because golf is such an individual sport. A soccer player can make an error and be saved by the goalkeeper, but a golfer knows if he screws up there is no one there to take up the slack. Fear plays a large part too. A golfer fears that a mistake is a sign of more to come. A baseball player thinks a mistake is an isolated incident. I often joke that only in golf can one bad shot be seen as a trend. A golfer can play eight decent holes, make one bad shot on the ninth and think, "oh no, here we go!" They completely forget the 32 nice shots made on the first eight and focus, deeply, on the one bad swing on the ninth. You can picture them, making their backswing on the second shot of the ninth thinking, "I dunno... this could be bad again! What if I hit another stinker? There goes my whole round, oh I knew it was too good to be true." It is true isn't it? And it really is not logical. I am not suggesting you approach the game all Zen-like, or like a robot. I am suggesting you approach it just like any other sport you play, and with a little less emotion.

You Use Golf as a Verb

Okay, this will not help your game much, it is just a pet peeve of mine. "Golf" is not a verb. You do not golf and you do not go golfing. No more than you tennis, or go baseballing.

Golf is the name of a game that you play. You play cards, you play basketball, you play golf. So, if anyone ever says you suck at golfing, you be sure to correct them and say,

"No, you're wrong. I suck at golf!"

You Buy Too Many Golf Books

You can see why I left this chapter until last. I do apologize; here you are reading my golf book and, here I am, saying you buy too many. Maybe this is the only one you have bought? If so, bravo. Read one more (*"Hit Down Dammit!"* by yours truly) and then quit.

There is no harm in reading a couple of golf books. (No matter how many you have read you ought to read *"Golf Is Not a Game of Perfect"* by Dr. Bob Rotella.) This chapter is addressing the person who is addicted to buying golf instruction books. Like Bogart. He buys one, runs out to the range to try what he has "learned" and when it does not work he tosses the book out, cursing and threatening to take up curling. Or, almost worse, he has a modicum of immediate but "uningrained" success and thinks he has found the Holy Grail of golf. He thinks he now has "the secret" and will never have to practice again, and sure enough, he quits practicing. Fast forward one month. New golf book,; same pattern.

Magazine articles are worse. Generally, if someone has gone to the time and trouble to write a golf book they have something they really want to say or teach. But, magazine articles? Imagine the pressure on publishers not just to come up with something new to say, but to come up with *dozens* of new things to say *each and every month*. Talk about re-inventing the wheel. Over and over again. For a living! The poor golfer - the customer - is the victim; subjected to a myriad of new, old, re-spun, often unproven tidbits of information, just wanting to learn a simple golf swing. Do you think it is in the interests of a golf magazine to promote the notion of a single, simple, golf swing?

Finally, (and then I will shut up about golf magazines) magazine articles do not go into enough depth to give you perspective on your own swing. The writer of the article has no idea what your "story" is. They do not know if you hook or slice, push or pull, sway or petrify, vote left or right. Perfect example: Bogart has way too much leg action in his golf swing. He makes Fred Flintstone's swing look composed. Bogart picks up a golf magazine at the newsstand. On the cover? "How to Use Your Legs More to Gain Distance". Bogart needs more leg action like I need more donuts. But, Bogart does not know that. So, guess what Bogart's swing looks like a day later? Put it this way: if he were in Vegas he would surely win the Elvis contest.

Staff:
"Golf course, may I help you?"

Caller:
"Yes, I had a tee time for this afternoon but I'm running late. Can you still get me out early?"

Other Books by Clive Scarff

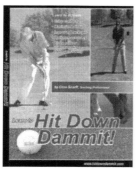

Hit Down Dammit! Teaches the concept and technique of hitting down at the golf ball. Available as a 4 DVD set, and book/ebook at **www.hitdowndammit.com**, **www.amazon.com**, **www.ravenrockpublishing.com** and other leading retailers.

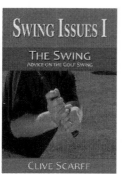

Swing Issues I – The Swing. A collection of tips and answers to readers' questions on the golf swing. Available at **www.hitdowndammit.com**, **www.amazon.com**, **www.ravenrockpublishing.com**, and other leading ebook retailers.

Swing Issues II – The Game. A collection of tips and answers to readers' questions on the game. Available at, **www.hitdowndammit.com**, **www.amazon.com**, **www.ravenrockpublishing.com** and other leading ebook retailers.

Thanks for reading *Why You Suck at Golf* and best of luck with not sucking anymore!

Made in the USA
Middletown, DE
19 November 2017